THE BLUE, THE LEANING-DOWN BLUE

First published in 1995 by **Salzburg University** in its series:

SALZBURG STUDIES IN ENGLISH LITERATURE POETIC
DRAMA & POETIC THEORY   **118**

EDITOR: JAMES HOGG

ISBN   **3-7052-0447-5**

INSTITUT FÜR ANGLISTIK

UND AMERIKANISTIK

UNIVERSITÄT SALZBURG

A-5020 SALZBURG

AUSTRIA

THE BLUE, THE LEANING-DOWN BLUE

PETER BEN JONES

UNIVERSITY OF SALZBURG
1995

For Joan, for Everything

ACKNOWLEDGEMENTS

to

Borderlines (Anglo-Welsh Poetry Society), **The Scotsman,** **Oxford Poetry** (Magdalen College), **Ayrshire Writers and Artists Society** (Diploma for Excellence), **Poetry Nottingham, Prospice** (Buxton, Derbyshire), **Quicksilver** (Fort Worth, Texas), **Avant Garde Award Anthology** (New York), **Iolaire Chapbook** (Island of Skye, Scotland), **Moonstone** (Settle, Yorkshire), **Outposts** (Kingston, Surrey), **Exile** (Saltburn, Cleveland, UK), **Encounters Anthology** (Peterborough, Cambs.).

CONTENTS

PREFACE

I used to think that there was much to be gained from probing into the notional thresholds between art and science – because everyone believed they really did exist. And because I believed they didn't. So the resultant 'complementary' world that opened up for me has been a rich preoccupation (and source of poetry) ever since.

Once upon a time, I used to keep telling everyone that they were artists, because 'the artist isn't a special kind of man, but every man is a special kind of artist' (Dr. A.K. Coomaraswamy). I say I used to do this, because everyone got very angry, telling me they didn't want to be artists. So I stopped doing it. But I still believe it strongly. I think.

But, again, there was a period when I kept saying (as I had once very cleverly written in an editorial preface) that there is a tendency for people to think alike at any given time. I meant it (probably -) as a reference to the influence of *Weltgeist*. But everyone seized on this obvious and axiomatic truism with such chattering enthusiasm, completely ignoring my very existence, that I not only stopped saying it because of being suddenly and completely isolated, but because, indeed, there was no need to go on saying it, with everyone else saying it. And besides, I began to feel ashamed of having said it in the first place. But I still believe it – I believe it in that first unsullied, pristine form I said it in. I believe it fervently. Yes, I think I really do.

So, in effect, you could say I have gone on saying 'nothing to nobody' for the greater part of my life, and so I'm the life and soul of every party (the ones I don't go to, that is). It's true, of course, that I have gone on writing, as, as Richard Aldington would put it, 'a sort of poet', about the things I have found out by 're-merging', as it were, the artist (sort of) and the scientist (sort of) in me, with all kinds of musical, philological and philosophical tools.

And whatever anyone else would say, I am glad to have had the opportunity, not merely to express, through my 'prism without walls', the very wealth that living has been, but at least to attempt that silent but most vital realization of its infinite simultaneities.

Even if (and 'everyone can write down names' –), even if I have stood, and relished standing, on the shoulders of everyone from Plotinus, Langland and Planck to Aldous Huxley and Sibelius: of everyone from James Joyce, Heidegger and Vaughan Williams to Professor Stephen Hawking, El Greco, Massinger and Mallarmé (for instance), with the most indispensable of Chinese Takeaways via Dr. Arthur Waley; even if I have had to stand on their shoulders to do this.

And was it worth their while, you say, to let him do this? His weirdly anciently-modernly lyrical thing – this mystically imagist-symbolist, science-revelling thing? "I think he's been trying to put everything in – to show 'everything's in the other'." Well, you're not so far off the mark.

It's been great, coming so close at the truth (with something very like it behind me), so close, that I've just seen it go by me, and I've had to keep going after it again. What a life, to be alive and have a crack at it all.

I must live in hope that there could be some others who might still get something out of hearing about the time of my life, in these ways (and when we're all, after all, so busy with the times of our lives), even though they might feel they've heard it all from me before – even before I'd stopped saying it, that is, as I've explained.

I did say they **might** feel they'd heard it all before.

Think of it as a contribution I made to a party by not being there. A variety that is the spice of my life; its continuum in every expression.

A YEAR TO CHRISTMAS

I caught the leaning-down blue in every glance
When in spring evenings warmth magnifies the trees with smoke,
And the walked path is soft with mud wafering flakelets
As cut cheese shears under the stalling foot:
The red sandix-like light spread upon cloud trees.
Then in oak forks nidulating folk murmured
Sleepy with the before-summer riband of rays
Before the spintharis chips pave the lake and the cauldron
Of the prying town frightens me: now
Hiemal armchairs flicker before the fender,
And with the sacred mentors of my child-life
Await, as I and the pampered hyacinths, the ascent
Of boon life-long decorations and sealing-wax incense, singing.

DIDN'T YOU EVER SEE ANY APPLES?

There is an orchard off a lane I know
Full now of sparkling leaves light-filtered through,
Yes, translucent leaves of emerald green, and the light
Rain can not be said to stay their warm
Stirring, or subdue the bright
Thistledown of clouds in their concentric storm:
For, with jubilant sprays, they penetrate to dance the lustre
Of the leaflet windows, glazing them in every shining cluster
Through blossoms ranged in posies round the crookéd apple wood.
In that sea of green and fluttering gloaming once stood
I, heard whisper of some further stream
Where the thin waters of this font divide,
And whence the sayings of her voice did lastly seem
To greet me (and which flight belied –).

There is an orchard by a lane I knew:
How dry of leaves it seemed that orchard grew!
For no longer did the paschal pleading
From the speckled satellites of birds distribute
Zephyred calls in leafy echoes, leading
Hollow, reed-like, to this grove: silent every thrush's flute.
But wait – I still hear the grave and luting serinette –
Not yet life-weary of its Spring – the cuckoo's canzonet!
Yes, now the overtones in this parure
Reveal it as undimmed, secluded from a sadness, to endure
Like the sweet timbre of the self's foretaste,
Freshening those scenes from any heat rays untoward,
And her, in whose loveliest mind and body chaste
I did true being glimpse, both here and afterward.

AS THE DAY IS LONG

It was all kind, so it was pasture, it was sky and pending

Measures of gladden-the-blue, blue was intending

In amongst the passion-fletched roses

The verdure bushes

Of love of the early world: o it was fresh

And mellow

Blowing and tor and culmiferous tufts and rushes'

Shares so keen breezed airy o moses

And azure bull-blow

Rubicund rivery pearly-round flesh

Morning swoons with milk rending

The billow-marbled gentle halo of my spring two doves:

Sight them, they are a-flying, still

They – dewed and pastelled as tender-brilliant morning:

See they ecstasy, æther green-light and gods, all delight

And euphoria, touch-horning

Exalted, touch forming the white

All-hands of me, all-over soft as fox gloves:

And out of these familiar silver

Strangers a first down whirlpool

Spiralled-spring-down, all that was lucifer

Striking as jubilant

Into every storm that it was other than cruel.

From: QUARKS AND HERALDS

Here's: all worlds of things
Adding themselves together in a planet-plant,
Taking thoughtlessness in their beginning -
Ending to existing
At either here and there
Equalities, and never in a day;
As in the pre-made mating
Of unparticled collusion
Lest otherwise the swink of time make lesion;
So they into the heavens' still rate must pour
Owing more than the beauty and loveliness of before
Which shall not therefore
Have ever passed away.

LOOKING ELSEWHERE WAXWORKS

I got this gaff that'll
Sleep six
Fat 'uns – and it was me
What saw the pepper
Ship blow up sky
High on the sealines
With the crocus-blasted fields
And frost behind me
And the sealions.

Empty windows staring all round my world
At my memory's fancy-free bags full.
It's a fact this world's a fiction
So it's made up of contradiction.

The more and more of looking back
And the more the no looking back of end approaches;
The starry-eyed skies a-blear
In our randomed atmosphere:
Moneyspiders falling out of my eyes
Now, specks that I saw more and more
In them before I died
As the smarting moneyspinners
That once fell out of my eyes.

So the plumules of the tippling stamens loom
Incumbent on the very Earth's gynaecium;
Consistent, weirdly private coloured shapes
And motions unfold with curiously dear
And intimate familiarity, continually within
The identity of self through life – .

– AND CURIOUSER

Call me
Churlish I half see
They stand in the hushed corners
Of their torrid bivouac's
High up place
Saying we can't do this.
(Night lights swinging from earthquakes,
Mokes tripping under precipice
Saddlebags, the hinny next
But one butts one).

A cat of crystal made
Immewed in the christmas snowflakes'
Memorable window,
A moggy purée-ing silver
Curtain slivers
Alight with seasonable-ever purring
Of whiskied smiles, while loving cupboard
Sodalites
Keep tabs on tibs
And still he tags along with flaky microlights.

Let us salute those whose winter died
While they were still filling in their donor card.
(Spring also has a quiet fulness
Which is perhaps greener and mystery-thicker than
A coming season).

BUBASTIS

A meringue coloured cat is my favourite cat
Though others may talk of a marmalade tibby:
But a meringue of eggs done to a light dun.
Still I confess to a soft spot for the ribby
Riff-raff of waif cats who winsomely run
With a raffish gait by the paling flat
Their caudal appendages straight up on end, ages
Roughly from nil to a thousand and one.
Honour the descendants, the noble empedestalled
Who hark back in their gypsyhood, royalty installed.

ANEMOGRAPH FLOWERS

When March is on the way
And the sun dies less early
The flat wind comes gusty
With a chalybeate bluster,
And the smell of rain-water.

All the world strides in contentment
In the hailstorm shower;
And with narrowed eyes
I breathe, supine, the rain's spray.
The sun dies, leaving the cloud ceiling grey;
Spring consolidates in the sprinkled heath
Gathering sensibly for the next advance.
A wagtail stirred, sang and bore on his wings
The wind away.

MYCORRHIZA ON THE HORIZON

I am the close fungus retrieving with far timber to root

I am someone I wouldn't be seen dead with, a bridle

Path walking over the gravesend of my body, Jones Davy

Before they tied up my victory in the locker slips

Longshot from dockyards in the Battle of the Nile

By Chatham and Pompey and Cleopatra's eye.

And England expects that this day the needle

And belaying pin, rattling and hawser

Of everyman will make the wooden ships

Into as-you-were forests from the chips to boot,

Every bit as good as before the longbow, and Pepys' navy, Sir,

Is trees again (but the sound

Of leather on wood is the Man renowned

Who once went before me barefoot).

SUI GENERIS –

A slob appointment with slops and clocks

No, I wanted dinner to be on time and not too late –
It was about six or ten past when I think about it
When my guests threw their soup back in my face
(It makes me blush grey when I think about it):
I just didn't know where
To look with this refund of slush
From every plate,
And I trod on an eyeful of stare
That wasn't there.

Well, I can't think that time's the thing to tell us,
So if we can only describe things as
The way they seem to be for us –
Like Einstein did and Newton did (of course),
Then I'm afraid that that's the way
They have to be
(Just for us,
Though, of course).

THE PÆAN THAT WAS A THRENODY

Now comes the burst of sun how warm!
Flooding across the bright green grass
So thickly bladed in matted swarm:
The hot beams through the curtain pass,
Its netting as a yellow rose
Shines blinding in the new-found sun;
On window panes the sun beam flows:
The silvered sky-blue Spring's begun!

Dazzling cream clouds creep o'er the roofs
Peeping between the solid tiles,
White stormy horses with dark hoofs
Gallop to keep with the wind's wiles.
Melting across my room the light,
Sharpened on course by flying air,
Minds of the moon one winter night –
Like milk. This day is warm and fair!

One recent day for my dear smiling girl I wrote
Below my signature (which she wanted me to write)
The date of that fast-flying day with his kind kiss.
But signing thus did I unwittingly commit away
All those happy days of past as gone for ever?
Of gardens, school days, streams and fields,
Of fragrant Christmas trees and roaring times
Before I knew this sunny lady? And when I'd
Stayed up late to watch the winter moon's eclipse
Through frosty panes with feathered flowers and silver ships?
(I'd read that night was ink the dream-man spills
To flood the sky and steep the paper hills).

But now – all these the music brings!

And time which passes, oh, so slowly –

Seconds, minutes, hours, with leaden sway:

Counting with such persevering pain

The tantalizing diminution till that day

When my life's spring-scented maid will come

And with the prophetic energy of the warm, reluctant sun,

Will seal my memories with her lips.

MUSIC FOR THE ROYAL EARWAX

Old showroom, old tearoom,

Hint of rummy what's it and do-da

Old jammy fingerprints of knick-knacks,

Footprints of impedimenta

In sandalwood or deodar

That we found on the road to Caersws

Via the Colossus

Of Rome

In a sunstruck howdah

And a moonstruck ha - ha

Under a calm Roman lampeter

In the flicker

Of a silvery simoom.

From: GENETHLIACON

Once
I went as far as the shore to the night sea
After I'd pressed through many and many a dark bank,
And I'd crossed dried-up rivers in the night –
The night whose moon was absent, softening
The waves to the blue stars:
I found myself on a beach
– I saw it through old walls
Of sea-edged windows:
O how I saw its night inviting, unsoothing lover!
Yea, in the day you were not mine;
And asleep it was not the sea
But you they kept me from:
They who made you, you again,
On Hero's Hellespont side:
They stopped me, saying: 'You may go no further'.

From the birth of days until their waning
Scaling the shipwreck face and the deadened sailing
Of songs, a flint-fouled petrel
Once a flower bird, failing.
As the days disburgeon, as the days gaining:
The people sent their bondage to the tree tops; and rifled
Was the pæan there and in the high well
Of the night-grey galaxy as it wrested; draining
Away from the land's affliction, the land's bastion flailing.
O the return, the still staved away return of world,
In the song the singing for it, not ever stifled
In the singing with the far farewell of wailing.
Of these things shall I tell?

If the scars of strain fall on me from this youth
Then life, leave me.

The mother, the sea, pernoctate the swooning
Of the wanderer of a kestrel, in its heavenwards falling –
Consuming the glory of the long desire.
Idées – echoing, echoing, palling –
Was the vision, reflection, drugged with foreboding,
The mirage of a fay to flicker away
Cruelly loving and cruelly beloved, in the mockery
Of man's pyre?

Over the head of this city the veiled evening unfathoms.
I conceive the constant undifferentiated sense
Various and informed through
My mensured, hodiernal, half-turn of half-century.
How many are the names of the beloved –
I can not span in my vagueness, powerless,
But they were many.

Let me not bear the burden of
The lines of face that smiling, taut,
At two-faced smiling of societal schist
Exacts: but if that split
Stony face is aught
There is, and that my love
Still persist,
Life, leave me; let me be, but not exist.

CORYDON IN HEIMSKRINGLA

Islands my Icarus has seen

White in a sapphire sea, and in the coral foam, white,

While upon the further land is copper richly laid,

Gilded and orange floating in light

Which can only come from the melting sun – :

For other I know not;

And where would glowing bars from furnace be

If in comparison they were set 'twixt heaven and sea?

How many dawns have risen in the Northern sky unseen

In desolate rift clouds and silver loneliness?

The sun for ever carried in white arms, paleous,

While men were sleeping in the kernel of the day.

The fields that slept were waking

As the flowers were in the wood;

The Earth fire-tipped in greenness

In the morning's twilight stood:

And nothing was there waiting for a dawn patrol like mine.

SAKES! LAWKS DE MUSSET!

When it could only just as well
Have not been heard, the bell in inland
Lhasa, from the outer forest trees
Deserted for ever in Northern Finland
When God saves by the bell
With the bumpy[1]Alexandrines
Of de Musset's *Mardoche*,
For an old relation's biodegradable
Body, unalien and shaven after all
By this tree's root grass:

At last on ancient liquids
Yellow as fustic wood more's the pity
With his bare teddingtons
In the glass roots glued
Beyond the celestial city
And the last decay-time kryptons.

Hephalantics and Aliphantics
Laughing all the way to kryena:
City the street, codfish-early with many
Midmorning grey wintry qi[2]
And choking with noisy
Traffic fumes, under the qiviut[3]-feeling
Light sweat of a fearing shirt

1. Reference to the dislocation of Alexandrines in *Mardoche*.

2. 'Chi': life force of Eastern religion.

3. Fur underside of animal.

That gets nearer and nearer

To the dentist mystery of gas alert

Up the stair to the chromium chair,

Warmly cold with an agonbite of Inuit feeling

When they cried in the wilderness, bred by far

Jamaican Inn-

Glish, saying Lawks de Musset, Sakes!

Put those patter-cakes out Alfred!

Gawd Sakes – Alfredo de Musset him

Have singed de bar-

bue[4]-riméd[5] fish cakes!

4. Brill.

5. Here one thinks of de Musset's masterful carelessness with bouts-rimés, e.g.

> Je suis depuis une semaine
> Dans un cachot,
> Et je m'aperçois avec peine
> Qu'il fait très chaud.

> (*Le mie prigioni*)

DAPHNIS, TO THE SUMMERCLOUDS

I see a landscape like a blesséd hope
And the sketch of blue above it;
The tree-tops, sighing, salve with us,
Faces of flowers revert to buds.

Ragged, torn, shining thickness –
White curved darker into sudden blue,
Colonnades of stately clouds
Stretch together at the hazy distance;
Ever brilliant of the sun,
Whose look makes the blue deep lighter.
No copy of a known thing
Existing without a thought
In their own domain
Of thoughts.

Blown along, obscuring azure:
Show bright convolutions
Of adumbrated white.
No gaze can see without a rapture
The wonder of the white clouds!
Fleece suspended, somehow solid,
With its smilingness, and blue,
Brings ideas, fleeting too,
Of warm flat lands, and yellow,
In another sun.

ON A FAVOURITE CAT FOUND AFTER TRYING TO FISH IN A TUB OF WATER

With acknowledgements to Mr. Thomas Grey.

Oh God – never a rain butt with paws!

Hang on, you're dead *right*! It *is* dead scarey –

It is our pussy who'se in there, blow me,

Though she seems not at all so hairy

Now she's absolutely soaking wet –

But look, she's still just moving, yet

It must be quite completely contrary

To all the natural laws – .

I suppose it's got to be a moderating lesson for us

Too, as well as giving puss

A salutary and thank Heaven

Not a drowning ducking,

To teach her, as you say, 'she really oughter

Not go on like this', chucking

All the birds out with the bird-bath water

Next, you bet you, because

She's sure to chuck herself out with them then

For good and all, and that would be a pretty pass

For puss indeed, for her

To finish in her natural sporting.

ACROBAT STAGED A COMEBACK

I set up my telespectroscope in Red Lion Square,
My spyglass to where
Marx used to march past with Engels,
Mooching to throw stones at the 'Far Right Fools'
Of the bloodgroups off Bloomsbury's Tottenham Court Road,
On the way to the Red Square of Lenin's Tomb
Way behind Les Invalides and the British Museum.

O – didn't you know they wanted to sell
Their Regency staircase and the eaves
(And their Adam ceiling) and the blue scenes
That Indigo Jones did of Reynard Keynes
Anointing the Muscovy ducking-stools –
From 'The Urns of the Rich and Their Privilege'?
And, I think, they were going on to include the first fridge
In the world: getting rid of it all (dehydrated and defrosted)
From their other mansion in Bloomsbury Square
(By just where one leaves
The British Museum corner),
To be reconstituted in a Milwaukee fun-fair,
Some Disney Jack Horner-
Land, like a Londoner's freeze-dried bridge?

But in the end that wasn't the chosen
Option, because they had a better offer
For the whole unfrozen
Boiling, to take out as well the Ten Commandments

Panelling, with its coffer
Frieze, and also the goffer-railed gopher
Wood Last Judgement dado –
The lot to be resurrected in a park for religious amusements
By a Leftist consortium of Born-Again Feel-Rights in Idaho.

I'm sending you this note (with these views
On the other side), although I don't need to,
In a bottle across the seas where we first met by St. Giles,
Because we had gone on meeting long before they said we had to.
When I saw your Tube rendezvous
Escalator (the one arriving
At our beginning lifestory's Tottenham Court rodeo),
It was then that you knew it was you and your reviving
And not just a future of recycled deals,
Of such arty fittings and rarefied vials,
I only seemed to take off my non-existent hat to.

From: CÆSAR'S NEXT AEROPLANE:
THE CAKE-TIME MACHINE

Have you ever sensed an object coming nearer

And as you stopped it

(– supposing you were eating cake)

You felt the time flow

Which would inevitably engulf the cake

While you were thinking about the object

Coming nearer,

Though it never stopped.

As it comes again

You lost by little degrees

The feeling you had before it went that little farther

And while you are thinking

The time you had apprehended had come:

The time, you were thinking,

Had eaten the cake

In the time you were thinking

And you imagine what the cake would look like

After you and time ate it

And at the same time

Had never completely or ever eaten it

(Your cake can have you, and as you eat it –

Though, of course, you never knew what each step,

And the end, would be like

Before you started,

Though there were no steps

And you never started stopping).

FULL FAIR OF FOREIGN FIELDS

Born to be drowned in the fire of London, satellite-
Linked when the cold front crossed Billingsgate from Finisterre's
Cape; all Froissart fed my unlearnéd London desk
While the bemused schoolday premeditated past life
Recurring, as a half-fright-
Ened phone phreak privily disinters
Memory stores of preordained futures,
Outflanking the classroom sunblind and the mumbled words
Of Latin, the quadrangle's greengages
With all their birds.

There, all Mallory and Berners, all Hakluyt (and St. Tom More)
Fed my incused
Desk, and came to it as well many a collected lesson-leaf,
And many a forthcoming secret bullet-
In and more than one hidden Dinky car,
While Dick's and Harry's sons, flicking ink-used
Blotting-paper messages,
With calm in their riotousness
Awaited our next war
With every pellet,
And the palpating pupil unfelt the palpitating feet
On the first pupated stairs.

　　　Show me the land where the wind has broken
　　　And the night immerses islands after sun and heather;
　　　O teach me again the crystal of the high moon
　　　For I have sheltered long ere now
　　　Where heavy trees wept on my childhood;

Whereupon the formative day left me,
Of heat, torment, wonder and fortune.
Eftsoon, come flora, come creature.

Lost in the shallows of eagerness
My wasting, wasted expectation
Tangy with the flower-favouritism of the bees:
From the too-much of influence
Agonies of trying, world without tears
Amen. Scuttering leaves shirred
The dormitory of frosts, the furniture
Creaks its story, and the chests relate
Very slowly the toils of a hundred years.

WHILE SHE TWISTED HER FINGERS INTO
THE MORTICE DEADLOCKS OF HER HAIR
(Homage to an unfrenetic winter reminder)

Sometimes it is a silver on black

Fetish out of the stream of in-to-out

Encountering fantasia, that is esoteric

Infuriatingness itself to hear and not to shout.

Only an aerosol ago on the road to rack and rune

I could smell the black aroma

From my first finger-denting pen holder

Nude in its descrying shame of japan lacquer.

Let me get back to this apparition, croisette

Over a wash-basin, pagoda of silver and black

Finial- and little onion minaret-

Trimmed shelves, overhanging and receding

In front of an ebony black inset filigree

Round the upright assiette

Of a mirror, all inside the shiny

Jet of spiky unfunerary tracery.

I begin now as then to voyage-glide,

And all in a Mediterranean summertide

Of noon, to fantasize nights around lagoons

Of black ice, in a 'Twenties opulence of simple emotional line.

There are fjords which the presiding ink-conjuror

Isolates from soap, amongst reflections of the outside

Clouds, lightly-oily pink on the negroid

Patina, where there are dream toiletries to be abjured

As it were by their own freshening disciplines.
It could all be of a starker roseate chill
In winter here or that I recall, but still
It is all unsuddenly acceptable, the niello mask.

A black moon shining in the big brain
Outside my head, the pillow trophies dauntless,
Of the tree clouds serene. Out of my time,
Always the most natural of all my ages.

A black sun shining in the ivory Kremlin splines,
God over us, I think fisherman apostles, formidable priests:
I think the opposites' feelings blend
And better themselves in the allowance
Of the others' forgetting that goes over my head.

LAND CHANGE
(HIGHGATE WEST HILL)

At first when the rain had passed I saw
The yellow ray upon the low ground
For the sun was down below the fields afar,
Bright orange-brushed clouds had seen him go.
Now the cold wind always brushes like a late flower
The winding and straight trees are black and misty.
Now clear the sky with the vapoury wisps
Who would veil the silver stars
Red in the west, white in the east,
And yellow fades to watery and white blue.
The convent and its turret-like near room
Nestle half-prominent in a cluster of trees
With the blue garment, the abstract bloom of winter air.
So parts of the building are indefinite lined
But cornice and parapet are firmly delineate
And eaves and shrubbery harbour secretly the child's magic.
Silent the wind and the bare sapling still:
Yet what is beyond the distance of those flat sleeping fields,
Past the near hill?

The lighted faces of moonlit houses
Like faces who were crying,
Tear-washed and pale: hiding behind slatted shutterings;
How the moon in her sky so graciously now reigns
Sudden seen appearing
Unawares through a clearing

Among the wet twigs, night holly.
But the vegetation and love redeem together
So that the stucco cottages welcome.
I see the moon whose embracing glitter
Catches the soul's breath;
Her scene strikes a memory of a pictured fable
Stricken between images of childhood and now;
The whispered fairyland falls on roofs illumined
Gently refusing the dusk-down.

EARLY NOSTALGIE: THE MOON IN WINTER
SYZYGY   (HIGHGATE WEST HILL)

I observe the lakes of the slatted grey
Through the intricate nets of twigs of black
And the huddling house framing with its varied roof the east,
The east of dark, of fuming calenture and maroon
Vision, the half-awareness of the battling moon.

Painting its peaceful flurry the gibbous discus sails
Amongst paintered punts of clouds in sky marsh shallows,
Close over the heavy-roofed convent whose kopje
Overgrids the vistas with its trees.

With unstrange bizarrerie the green serein moon
Buoys in the chill steaming sea over the housetop slates
Of the westering hill, while the white fungous smoke vacillates
To vanish and re-appear along its now more fevering lobe –
Now staring upright in its eastern sea, near inshore running
Like the vertical ocean of day, as you walk down to the shore
By a hill and the horizon is above you, and the sun
Roars in the drowning blue.

(As if from a ship I saw you, balanced geminal
On either side the waves;
Where were you then, Selene? Hoist with Pleiades,
Or in Neptune's lighted caves?),

Once more I saw the moon, a minute later, full round between
The house and the church, over the last house, below the next
Steep house – its night red roof and yellow stucco dim walls:

The bulgeless globe fluttering low by the roof, the wall, effulgent.
In the immense distance to the sky and the flat-spread sky
Bordered by the church, the steeple, the bastions and bulwarks
Of trees in the church-yard: gas-lit green round the thin monument.

Behind me the stars skipped, ailed not, in the fillets of blue,
Beside the poaching, inflating moon, shining from deserted windows.

THE SHAPES OF TIME

Found again just before twenty, I saw
Under blossomly walls of a birthplace the high folly
Peaks of alps of snow once more, in yellow-green silent
Shouting leaves betweenly: the cloudland's playbox
So shining! I thought – so many icings twisted on my cakes,
That wonderfully come with all of them, and sadly
Without them deign to go.

Egging on the face of my tapering spill
Are the columns of lost friendship, joined in fractured sights;
But then ago I was all six of me
Still a life of undercover fraudsters,
And full of unwaiting frolic I was for ever
The defector of all a shamed composure's rites.
Then with all things lovably and vilely
Guiltily visible I felt
I felt I was the wonder of my age.
And après moi le Delage.

Loopy fretted banjo faces, holes round the commutators
Of ozone-singing blue-sparking dynamo casings; patent shoes
And pouty prudish flirts on band boxes, mouth organ fronts
Of jalopy bonnets with chromiumed intestines of manifold
Exhausts, glinty-grey honeycombed radiators sported by Buick
Sedan cars (and the common affordship's flighty flivvers),
The superior geared-up whines of Renault's snobbish cabriolets
And Bugatti's: all chugging and bearing-down radiators; page
Boy cuts and bulbous intimidating shiny perm machines in

Parlour windows; curvilinear cinema frontages, openwork wire-
Lesses, their smelly ebonite half screening a proud clutch
Of red glowering filaments limber in glass valves. All these,
Airstreamed, streamlined, airsmoothed fine rattling things
And sleekened things, apparently after Blériot and Farman
(And Blaise Pascal, for that). But après moi le Delage
Was the wonder of my age!

I seem to remember when they were not so squeamish
(As in those early surgery cartoons), about inserting
A Doge's grand canula into the monseigneur in Venice
For a canine resuscitation: I don't think I am mistaken
Any more than with all the other memories that enlarge
Before and after me, as après moi le Delage.

THE MICRO-THRILLER OF A LIFETIME

The Charge

This is the most beautiful day of my life, she said,
And then he shot her dead.

The Evidence

I'd so much want to find a home
In the grey country or neat
In a town neat street
With I think snow ivy the one and a smallish lacy pane
And perhaps wet privet outside the other I think, after rain,
Where there must be the calm indoor
Festive bustle building imperceptibly
More restfully anticlimactically
But not unlike Christmas eve, and mutton for
A meal, meals, to link, in a muffled chink of excite,
A window fern and the china ewer
From yesterdays and the bedroom's linen and white.

The Plot

I heard the old army's cry fade
Like all the roar of a lost civilization
As, inquisitively scraped with spade,
A pot piece moved, seeming itself the cessation
Of many days heaped together in a yesterday shade.

The Whodunnit

Once that was all hustle, raucous and imperious and craven
Too, now undifferentiated amid the desultory dust's
Gulping relics (it seems, so it seems).
So it is after that us who looked through one
Another, lacking even a pretence of sympathy,
A flash of loyalty, new springing – , when we were young.
I hear again as I saw again
An eternal dry leaf outside the youth's starry-
Opaque bathroom window, moving in the frost afternoon
And evening smart breeze of a birthplace town, still considerable
In the calmer keen wind of winter, in the bright north London blue.

The Verdict

This is the most beautiful day of my life, he said,
And then she shot him dead.

DEATH OF A FLUTE

I am walking through the snow towards Egypt
In the colourless serenity of the livery of stars,
For the runaway of forests with limbs of timber
Stained the cortège of my birth
When I was so sudden a soul.

They said it was not as if one day he did not wake
Because the vapour of the tumbling airs was new as earth:
But in pursuit of a dream his world waded out;
So where is fame that loves when we are gone?
My time is but azure and the seconds are termites.

I am tired of thinking my song spread before all man;
Forasmuch the pavane of naiads mourns the poet's elf,
Bedridden in the miller of the dreaming self –
That peace which is to be breathing as the seas asleeping.

One day I shall not be quite able to place you;
Spring is in bluer clouds I spy by the curtain side.
You too can with goddesses of the green fates play
And the yonder spirits of the waters' way.

THE BLUE CONVICTION

For, as he sees the Lord
present, equally everywhere,
he does not injure his true
Self by the self and then
attains to the supreme goal.
Bhagavadgītā
S. Radhakrishnan

Plato; *Timaeus*

Yes, that sky's blue and deep

But I can't know what truths those vaults secrete

And yet in me

I know that I am part of Thee

(– Thou heavens outside and I are One).

There is no I to stand alone.

Scintillating points, a myriad in the Dome above

As I gaze I know that I

Am of the One in love.

And all I feel around – this tree –

Tell me they are part of me,

There is only I to see its greater Self

And so beholding beauty

At length be One itself.

Our peace of mind, outside us as it seems,

Initiates the ends of all unknown things;

And all is symbol, generative in itself

From all the incidents of life

Which go to make eternity.

AND THE ONE AFTER THE NOT REALLY DONE-TO-DEATH GOLDEN OLDIE   (THE OLD PLACES OF CHILDREN)

A fate worse than

Death to find yourself alive

When no-one knows what it's like to die?

The labels you stick on your unlapelled self

Can only say you didn't make it

As the underlying labels say

And they don't lie as far as we can see.

Sometimes you might be led to think

There are too many planets on this person

Growing out like medals of leucocytes –

All home movies of the lovable characters:

Families waited upon daily by Vlaminck (and

Betelgeuse) and Modigliani,

All the night burghers and proselytes,

All cat buglers and propagating greenhousemen

(With shagreen phalanges –): all dead air drinking.

Some would say now, that all

This calmly green and unthreateningly coolly

Roominess, of snugly low ceilings and low-shot middle distance

Views – , was light years away

From the green of horrifying lying-in-waiting

Inescapable suffocating operating rooms,

All torture-prisons of somehow ultimate my-betterment

Of here-or-there blessèd release prisonments.

They would be right; only in that

In the after-convalescence of seeming trial or peace

The instance and the memory are outdone

In one unresisting, one unwanting-to-resist,

Where only mere peace, – and horror, don't belong.

Terrified child, of even then nightmare creative

Experience, realizing and jacking-up reality;

Oh yes, and a child of that older, knowing at least all that

Or less with more: knowing always that all that is nearer

And not even come what may –

Even after the solatium of severe reminder,

That some dull-dust sparkle comes

In the still warm after dawn bright,

Before the full heat begins its away of flight

In all the freely-praise of daydoms – :

And then I must have rested fear

In the midst of away-known cold of terror –

So many younger and after sling-surges

Of trying desperate now for undesperate after.

The child that remembered the other-same garden

On the silver of an endless beach, low

Into mauve distances, somehow

By trees and not truly distant seas:

There then they were with him bothly,

It was all sky lulling and quietly

Light, like silk impending,

Like sleeping midsummer's Christmas snow.

In the delightly nursing gut of feeling

I knew I was in the whitely and rose

Sand-floated and saltly

Mist childness on the home-near shore

As was on the home-far Spanish shore as near.

A-BYE ROCKING CHAMBER

Cream of ivory   cygnets sleeping

   On the fairystory   grotto stream

      As the gliding halls   slowly in gypsum

        Make the eyelids   of the sun child

         Momently open to his future   under the re-covering limes

      And he becomes   asleep again

In the pass   of the little swans.

NO WORSE FOR IN THE DRINK

These sternsheets, that deserve another

Old sailor's spliced mainbrace

Like the frosty ale on the face

Of the far-flung Dover Patrol, O'Slaffery

It turns out; fretting yourself about buying a drink

For this mouthpiece of all the denizens of the stokeholds

(Like a rich man worrying himself sick

Over the encroaching inroads

Of the colour of his chauffeur's livery):

Who burnt and froze under and above the corvette's

Waterline while in my unescorted convoy I masoch-

Cringed under the debating Heinkels for months on end:

They also serve who only lie in wait

Not only faithly to walk one unthought day

On the peaceful Giudecca quay

By the sloppily bell-strewn and inseparably

Beloved Canal Grande

But, just as if it were I who was with you in the tanks at Cambrai,

Wait for the saving Tipperary

Sailorman to come back via Greenock

From Murmansk, without his minesweeping share of the spoils

Except for the paravane glory holes

From a crippling shell to a legabout

To go on and get the cryosurgical boot

By the cold shouldering of a bomberless Leicester Square

When not even the old hearts and flowers are there.

NOW YOU CAN DRINK AND DERIVE
(Today was the day before yesterday)

I see myself coming out of a dark-suited cathedral
Where there had been some sort of wedding involvement
(And I know I should never have killed myself);
The sky is louring like liebestod Sunday
And the people who will soon all go away
Even so make the moment lastingly sticky.

There is a lode, one of a myriad, where our starting had not time to stop
Within the lodestar's timing, pointless-guiding;
Now, at long-short last, the only thing I fraughtly-laden know
But nearly know, is that meaning is really outside me biding,
That that reality of heavens that started my stardust outcrop
In all non-starting – up-taking the forfeit of my time of flow –
Is out-not-out there, and all my gropings for a meaning
Only but sublimely rest in the sharing-knowing gleaning
Of that meaning, not my knowing meaning merely.
And this praying-feeling, I come there-from,
There-here-exist and go thereto, in stilly maelstrom
Undirectionly.

(Every September I hear the intricate proud whine of Merlins
Machining, their shadows of wings contend with cowlinged Benz,
And a boy confusedly confident under massed vapour trails,
High shell bursts or staccato cannons,
Runs home from school to beat
The falling shrapnel and the ominously-ending wails
Of the howling siren at the end of a swain's North London street).

Even in Shropshire, now, I can still see a star
In deep blue between
Low night pink chimney pots
Outside the dark white window frame,
Still like late night Toytown.

What are my dead thinking, they long-dead familiar,
As tonight I eat my yet-again honey –
What because of that iteration think they of me – ?
Will they say, go along then, it all brings us this way?
As I cut the cornermost tasting of the cheese
It has become the tastiest morsel of all the cheese house.

SOME (LONG? –) TIME AFTER THE BOMBARDMENT

(Midges seen through the telescope of a cheese-stick)

On my birthday nobody will ever be
Any older than when I first knew them –
They the slight friends would never know me
Again, not least after my terrible mixture
Of living; and there were always those who would
Never have remembered me either. In the teeming midges
Of us shall I still use the guided images
Of my system against all invaders, to be non-invaders?

I don't ever want it to be later than Easter,
With the piercing blue triangles peering high up
Smelling of starch in the lovely atrocious summer
Garden; under the railway girders to above-between
The two above me black steeples in front of the blaring sun.
Poor ditties percolate, pitch, perfect pitch
In this dark world of sun.

There it is ominous even in the country's town
Because the sun-blackened pavements are the same
Of stuff as behind the redoubts and retrenchments
Of North London grubby squares; and I stagger breathing
Hopefully the broken promises so peerless in sundown.

It is time to look at the picture with the moon
In it again, as I almost think of a banal
Figure against the subliminalities of the Brahms
Double Concerto. A bird suddenly screams out, struck
By the thought of a frightening dream-moment
In its sleep of trees; I find myself groping
Like one grateful and cruelly blind, abandoned amongst
Like simple strangers, in turn emergingly glad to be kind.

WHERE HAVE ALL THE LOVE LIES BLEEDING GONE?

Why should I hit you Jack
Pot, you know I never do
Make a killing not even
A big one when my number
Comes up to one, not two:
Trying conclusions with one who
Doesn't know my weakness,
Not loved for weakness, a
Sharing one, for a start
And a finisher,
Loved not, so; loved, no.

And when I hear the poet
Of a man's wreck cry like a lamb
Out of his destruction like
Less than the artistry of a babe
(Somewhat like this my dithyramb) –
A man like the man who died
With his gift, except this one's
Gift died while he lived.
Oh I'm still never a last one
To presume on denying the lone
Valid light of any silent cry.

He's slipping away, the lifeless frazzle
(I *did* think, afterwards –),
All coercion to a writing escritoire or two:
Mindless in the bog of death and bobbydazzle
Who wouldn't have the pale memories of bedrooms:
Wouldn't you?

MOUNT HUON, PICARDY

These graves, but forgotten and alone,
Though so neatly kept, poor white regiment,
Small rows out on this spring plain,
Simple, exposed to lark, windward trees and snow;
You all died in agony long ago.

But as I think the minutes and years
Must be unbearably long to your stillness
So now your time of aeons only lightly bears
And rather do your removed spirits
Pity our heavy, faithless minutes.
We gassed you and relied on our forgetfulness.

I AM SOLDER TO NECKAR AND AM BRAZIER TO SWABIA

I was once locked in Olympia
In its subterra labyrinth under the exposition
Halls full of gawping natural gazeteers (yes, I was one),
With the former gas dump demilitarizer of the Neckar
And lately keeper of His Majesty's Government
Ammunition Arsenals – deadly arsenicals in old leaky-
Sealed gas weapon cramps at Waltham Abbey
Clamps, he told me, he told captive audio-me
(et ego in Orcadia quondam),
As we tried to scale the forbidding lattices
Of doors over the padlocked bars, out of just as obsoletely-
Out of over-there still gas-filled and forgotten
Sappers' traps. So not so long ago as ago I was infantly
Again lost under this Mount Olympia's parapets
I was one of the countless nuclear
Fallout families of only children
Stranded and so much out of the faceless
Press that this stray one played before all of them –
A favourite spectacle, after all, in the holiday
Eldoradodom of an advertising spade-and-sandpit!
They were all in here the same then
During the pointless vogue of the Ideal Homes: yea
We were all as good as welded in the wistful thwarting
Rhine-side river – unwiseacres, all us before and coming
Creatively breath-poisoning enemy-echoing-
Heidelberg men. I don't so much know if I and my stuck-with

Essexually Swabian Inspector just now got out from
Under that exhibition still-homelessly scrambling
Any more than we all got out from that earlier childly
But not really before exhibition I made of myself
For them then, if we got out then as now
As I desperately fancy, via the sweet air, from us –
From selves of old and young gasmen, via the sweet air
Of staircases from deep shelters –, dugouts,
O did I too get out degassed and unguiltless
From my terrible gasmasters of mustard and nerve gangrene,
From jobs like leering useless wars, so did I get out
Empty of them, guardians and jailors and all, back
Into the stars via the sweet air.

NEWS FROM THE MODEL WOODEN
GEARBOXES OF UNCLE WILL

Over the cripple's minuscule gasring him
Gasping with his roll-your-owns, his shadow
On the window, conspicuous
Said, 'Widowerhood?' And once more, with limping
Breathlessness, a favourite theory was but partially explained.
It would always come right to 'have it meet you', as ordained,
And not to have it 'ready made'.
Can it always –.
I remember the flaring bit was put into the solder
At that stage of final Q.E.D. (there was a wireless tuner for repairing),
And if I wanted to hear any more of such grown-up philosophizing
I should have to wait till I got a little older.

Well, it was those, his craft-things – after *her* viduousness
Of him who'd stood agonized on artisan's crutches or sat
In that back workshop offering his arthritically cramp-macramé'd
Carpentry mechanisms of hope in others' daimlered days
While his days had pained –
That they gave me – to killjoy them by my own hand – the child
Who would only live to write them off (unbelievably to cherish),
Till and unless they could think what else to do with them
(The gear change was the smoothly clash
Type, of the segmented gluing of cedar cogs precisioned
Like turbine blades).

And between schooltimes and after school times
It gave me to think afar again: I saw his all-black horses' plumes
When I came to the house of the lunchtime funeral,
With outside it the jet-black hearse;
I overheard noddingly animated talk about just how much
A nice wooden gearbox would be likely to fetch
From patent agents with outlets into the design trades.

And then I knew that, well before the teapots and scones
Of the last never-goodbyes, those nakedly exposed, bereaved Master-
Sculptures would be ever so prayerfully retrieved
From me, in all the dead live-fingered working of their woodenness,
In exchange for a No.3 Meccano Set, with much faster
Cog wheels (so they said, and after school next day), in a vastly
Better disposition of the assets ('It really would have been *too* ghastly'),
Within my callow earshot they went on to wheeze,
'If he had ruined their entirely unsuspected, lovely
Value – like if he had smashed them up – : we're so *relieved*
It dawned on us as beneficiaries to make
The best arrangements in the light of mourning lunch and teas
And in the nick
Of time, and so the boy won't be so grieved
With any *dead* belonging –
And as Will himself would like, poor thing').

And then I also knew that, through the dreadful funeral breakfast, breaks
The trust of a wonder of work,
Made long before the moment of death,

So to keep the pain-wrought makings

Of a life far away from any price of takings,

To where the maker's life still finds and feels.

Whatever seems the fateful route his leavings take

Through rapacious plans and dirgeful wake –

Even then I think I thought –

And in prospect of the No. 3 Meccano Set –

It must be that near mute fidelity and watching share that really carries

Our box of toothed and crutchless wheels

Away, to stay with those of us

Who only appear to be laid in earth

(After so many deeply respectful burial lunches and interment-breakfast

teas).

EGOTRIP MEMORY

For a life time moves and there is still again;
Yet time is my follower and pretends,
Setting an attitude to staid formation, voice and strain,
Yet to be variant as life and as life without ends.

That jaded thespian which the promised child
Becomes, refers, as does the child, to older dreams
Which, like the nursery forms, behind the times
Brood in a constance that protracts familiar rhymes
Which are as known and as secure within the just-past, smiled-
At comfortings as in the infinite soul not writ in reams.

INSTANTONS

I was an officered boy with makings of tea (put a sumpsimus in
The brew so the leaves read out better), that tippling tea I was
Tipped in as a Lipton apparatchick, a booked boy going for
Gold I was good as not making – , and miseried never to have a
                                                        bonanza.

By night time with putti chasing in the overpanels
I thought long before after-ethered days
Of hospital children's transplants it is no good
Even thinking of a brain transplant one day when there
Is no money put away for it and they won't even let you play
With the other infants' toy animals, and tonsils are all the rage
With febrile adenoids (and then you aren't even a child any more –).

Organ tissue compatibility could only refer then to my old
Aunt's velure thighs on the velveteen music stool, pedalling
Her harmoniums she was never even in the bread line
For a corrected mistake and kidney machine therapy,
When they forgot too late to open her up again in Southend
To look for the calliper-forceps they lost, when they didn't twig
The killer sight of a staring spleen they afterwards said
(Post mortem) had been pitching back fermenting urates
And which must have been at first vision
Just asking for excision.

That was the state of tissue affinity knowledge then, that
And the rogue forceps, that beat the surgeon, crossed the last
Of Aunt's pyloric doorsteps (and that was well before
The rapture of the unexpected gossip

Of a guipure underslip –
Well after Aunt Katie last opened her diapason stops
With a bitten under-lip).

Well I was forced back to the resort of calabash paintboxes,
To watercolours of splanchnic mesenteries only seen in accidents
And cats'-meat shops. It was when I stumbled upon the possibilities
Of a steam jet piped from water boiling in an old sweet tin,
And blowing back from my trolley, that I remembered with advance
Nostalgia the after-pistons that would silently sign my failure
With the jet discovery at the end of the coming war.

It was then as much as before
I was born that I sensed all over again that it was the instantons
That clicked it all in and out of place, while it stayed in place,
All at once, and made the time match across all space, when
Really time had always faded out with space, when our sight
Had become properly blinded with basics, and cepheids and absolutely
All the vacantness of impedimenta were everything.

IF OUT, TRY AFTER MESSIER 3

I am here! ('Is there

Unintelligible life out there?'

'Yes, it is like this here

As well as worldly-same'). Here I am in a freedom trap

Of stars, which would be only called

A man-trap, if it were not more

Horrible-wondersome by far

Than earthmen can tell to earthmen just like that,

And not be able to abjure the fear,

The constant life of capture

And reach out to more than wonder, even; not be able

To tell in grim shape-thoughts,

Other than in terms of the besetting pictures cast

Of what they themselves have done

And not what those taken to the stars become.

No, I am thus incommunicable

Life out there

Ablaze with unutterable words

Coming across comets that are part of me

In an already rencontre

As in the timeless void, the interstice worlds of makeweight maps

Which really fill the stars' apparent empty gaps.

The bread that made my body

Made it voltage-prone;

My day, a thousand bloody sweats

Of what it was,

Broke me by that bread alone.

White, that is the all-seeing eye;
The bread that broke my body,
That bread I broke,
Was just as white as it was bloody,
And my dying wine was turned
From red to living white.

I could not tell the time anywhere unless to say
As it were in the power and essence
Of placeless timelessness
(So much for cosmic clocks; do
Leave a note if I should seem to be out
After all – I'll leave Space for a few words, anyway).
Watch this space – .
O here they can leave
The soap in the bath
Unless they don't want to,
If there was any soap (there is), and were any
Of them (there are). There is an anti-bath as well,
Of course, and anti-soap, for not having to keep clean
All the skinless wonders.
And here you can elevate your jealously protected loves
In the privacy-trained truth of spacelessness
(And not give them away, lowered from exquisitest passions
As every one else's are down there – diminished by being too open
Rather than being fired by being enviedly unseen –).

A DAY OUT ON THE TOMB

I take it for granted as when the impulses first
Flowed down my arm to this tingle of finger
And the urge to screwdrive and build or watch and cry
(Or with precaution that this be crippled and suffer
With impressed patience to death, before the overjoyings of to die);
And I pass out to the rising and outmoding
Culture comedies of rackrent and ruin,
All my formative shuffling shabby-from-influences:
Waiting for comics and the next science magazine
As the balloons went up, just as the zeppelin had
Over the hoisted baby's head,
And one wonders how it was ever accepted that one read.
And so without the absurd honours degrees engraved on,
Indecencies of the naked headstone,
Each of us if the validated birthdaysuited mason
That put his eternal finger on the wait
Till I'm decent again gallantry
That unstops the gargoyles of unearthly gain
Not spouted from the chapter house roof's chantry.

NORFOLK SHORE

That's more than my job's worth to the power of n –
When I was on the road to Emmaus
You used to meet 'em.
I remember a night when a shining ear of corn
Out of a singing field made me gasp with sense
Of unanger, as at a mixed metaphosphorescence,
Like with the praise-worthying of a new writing's
Dwelling place. Thus the corn conveyed to me its germ.
It was, I remember, while the hen
Pheasant negligently
Beruffled her be-gathering broodery, and gently,
All tan-tawny by the Paston road;
And the sea came up imbued with feather-fiery colours
Just like the gushers from the undersea,
And I was turned on
As in a halo of this and that instrumentation.
And just for that nonce in a vale very
Close to the anciently Edingthorpe spire
(And thencewards to Norwich and Colonus via
Every Baedecker raid you ever dreamed of, every coach
Party from the cathedral city to this shore),
I saw an angel-man look over my shoulder
To another lightness I was also suddenly walking with;
And then we both realized (or I did)
That this all-lighted one's approach

Was not so much to let our

Bright be in his infiltratedly shade

But show that he was one of us who had

So unshadowly made

To be outside us – but infinte-more than the sum of us.

For at that point I saw

That beforehand had the suns and stars lit up his nimbus,

Like the windmill was on fire here with all its river of corn,

And I was privileged to walk on as if he hadn't only seen us

But I had seen them both and more,

The rapport

With him beyond thought of wonder-scorn.

SPACE PAINTER

If you could gyp the stallion who trounces
The black rents of the galactic smokes and flounces
His mane in the simulacra of space flowers,
Then his hoofs would gunmetal and shy the overworld,
Mounting his huge galloping amongst climbing
Of Spirits who rose out of Thebes and Arcady;
And ironclad Vulcans in the niello portholes of dawns
Would fade ashen and reluctant to show
Gangways of greaterness and spouts of Thrace.

And thence Sennacherib, from out the ironshod
Battering, comes hustling stringencies
In clumps of stars like eyeballs out of place;
And the Senusrets threaten with the hobbling
Bilboes of the vault's outdome,
For the starlight issues from a curvetting fetlock
As the hammered nostrils of chasms
Are shanked by the steed's flanks flung
By the fending foot-ram and the moon-breath foam.

GADARENE'S WINE

A high-tech real fantasy surveillance
from the lays of Ancient Rome.

From Caracalla in his the bath to the saddled

And scrubbed likeness as Marco Aurelio, in Campidoglio – .

By the vintage decanter and the halved

Pineapple, the 'cakestand' semblance –

Up there in the Villa Borghese

Across remains that were the Viminal's – :

This camouflaged verse word-processor

Disposes various futurenesses,

While the databank got up as a

Chafing dish waits

To be carved

With cognitive hammy breadcrumbs from an infra-

Red jetting armchair, which is browsing how many bytes

Can take it through two millennia

To a random ride by a ham (egghead addled)

Hacker with fibre optic lanyards.

Without any one being any the wiser, or any J.S.

Wagner having to profess his Venusprobe Music virginals

On the Kurfürstendamm or in Tooley Basin Street (Borough).

So thence, en route, Adonais is detected falling over

Up the Spanish Steps towards The Spaniards

(Yes, it is, it *must* be! Keats disengroves

From the Eternal City to drink his Vale of

Health, serenaded and abetted by Seychelley (Mitsu-

Bishi) Percy – an oriental Hotspur).

And yes it is here
White lilac in heavier
Bunches than ever, You
Dreamt I had written as
If what I had written in Venezia
Had overheard limpid Debussy coming from a piano
Embarked in a colour-light garlanded gondola.

And in the dank dugout the latest
Unsighted avant guardsman, in disco inscrutably
Slipped, or meths hangout, garden party or privy parliament,
Indolently threw up the valour vocabulary of the exact meaning-
Catching of their languidly corrupted off-key words, dead-
Spitting their image-age; what else?, when they, the conglomerates
Resignedly say goodbye and leave, what do you do? How are you
Supposed to manage alone – ? Unless, unbeknownst to them
It then becomes more powerfully easier in you – .

From suggestive shenanigans amongst the raunchily anthropoid
Pepys-like goats: you were born to be the man the man interceptingly
Mistook you for in Yarmouth (I.o.W), that you needn't here avoid –
Forgotten like the other one in Oxford Circus
That also (*now* you remember) said, baldly censorious,
When you think of genius and alopecia don't forget Sibelius
(But none of the fostering few helped your legs to fly like this
Before you took away the legs their walking taught to arrogate).

But you forgot the man, also – ? – unspeakably profligate – ?
Who said he was Sid Ballyass, whose skilly of osmosis
Penetrated all the Pohjolas and Lemminkäinens with interferon-
Like cold soup. I wonder if there is room on the screen
For more unseen lines to carry a superceefax of Sibelius, *The Oceanides*
To underline the subliminal I am prolifically with face lines
Quite aware of now, I think, pushing a pauper's tumbler
Of undrinkable Falernian from Catullus to Horatius Flaccus
Into the pigs of song, into and out of carminative facsimiles,
And my attenuated bull calf's approaching gore becomes
The takeaway veal of the most asthenically anorectic of bulimeys.

QUEER OLD STREET

I got my cheaper (and more and more cheaper made)
Suits from a friendly bee as a busy
Jew inside leg by Warren Street, tailormade still when
I was working in words about resin wesley
Rocket weapons of spun glassmanship
In Epworth Street in the fringe
Of furniture woodmen of Hoxton
And Shoreditch, honourable artillery gentlemen
Of roundheads, Milton and Bunhill Fields
Areopagitica pamphlets pasted on the walls,
All are still so crannied with freshly lost weeds
Lasting in me long before the pikemen before Wellesley.
And before they were a twinkle in a bird's-eye
Patterns, feeling my pasterns my suits went seat-shiny.

MY MODEL OF MY PICTURE OF MY PAINTING IN WORDS

As you were plying with deploring cocktail cherrysticks
Found in the old tantalus in a long line of tricks:
Persuaded so, I first painted and then
I wrought this doubling lantern
Of harlequin film to hang Klee-like
Appended as a leaded-
Windowed lamp, lit through red thermidor
Plastic paintworked sheet in frames-of-wire.

From some other morello cherry's flame,
Light-locked-up by crafty manufacturing tangs
Of hands, their lobster-claws
Like twisting tools with forging fangs –
Shaping signets I could unwind from round my little fingers,
Unwind and turn and tease
Into transmuted stiffening alloys,
Sculpted skeletons from plans and concepts.

So I got my memory's Hampstead Heath from that decanter
Under Great Aunt Thyrza's thorium burner-
Bright (she I always had no patience for,
Who once too always saw
That mantle's micro-waffling blinding-white,
Heard the lowered guttering gaslight's greenish suss-
Urations, over the chipped and browned enamel
Beetroot underlings of the bubble-and-squeak dishes –
Alongside the smoked-plate moons
All above the mantleshelf's fringing bobbles,
The Shantung silk puffed-up doubloons).

For me a nightlight owl and neverletgo gobbles
Are forever lambent in that gazed-into gazebo; and thence is hence,
A dream that delights you to bed
With scheming aforethoughts for no-pence.

SCALED-DOWN POLYMERS

I am the uselessly sponsored polythene bird-scarer
That at the crow-tame table scaffold
Of PVC impregnated plunder-seeds
(Packed in ozone-friendly CFC polluting ecospheres)
Raves in the water-repellant meadows
Every morning. You only have to get out your old
Rag and dress like a corvine scorpion
In your silicone dusters of ragabone clothes
Blasé about natural disasters that take
Your nearest from you, your dearest disaster:

When they, after our kind, find their fibre
Content more with Millais
In place of your all-bran Ruskin
Who has gone to seed
And while they still have time for
The healthfoods of loving need
In any conveniently ruttish côterie and melée
(Along with the leering, randily brassy and brashish
Belgian holiday women
In their short black plastic mackintoshes
Who, escaping from husbands done in
With Stella Artois and hashish,
Also make no uncertain protestation
Of their love-labours and their fruits
And that they are carrying polyurethane
Torch-holders for other suitably plasticized partner-substitutes
But not for you they ain't –
You're too much of a dumb mini plastic saint).

THE UNERRINGNESS OF UNCERTAINTY

Out of the immanent cistern, perspex locks
Of my picksome improbability garner-granaries,
I asleep raving run my myriad dreams' canaries
And dredge up the most unlikely keys
That are to be the measure all anew, reams and flocks
I always felt there more than fickle theories,
More like un-dreamt-up sonnets of the dark lady
Coming out (eventually) from the typing monkeys.

Rough ridden over the rubbled rollers
Of my basemost mind's great feast
Emerge the no-chance chummages that are
Alone true yet again, and not nearly such alien strollers
As it might seem, at first at least,
That they must be; no, they are strangely familiar.

NEVERENDSKY

Stay with me, willy nilly, lively remains:
How much have I seen things to change –
Even me, across these years, ageing
And suddenly, anew, youngly different?
Even me, snatching at crumbs of petty
Very local, very vulgar fame.
In the long run, too many loving weaknesses
Were at work by half. Like the priest who sexually
Assaulted the bride during the wedding ceremony.
God knows what you thought you were
Letting me in for, when you bore.

Having confessed our faults
Put in with philological inexactitude
The hand to touch beyond the words
Having to touch our thoughts.

It was Rachmaninov playing with snow
Across the Nevsky, there was no doubt
Arose, the arpeggio'd sound was a visor which survives
The chant of our laborious travels, our irksomeness,
Always looking out from the eternal page, as did
Piano acciaccaturi on Firenze's Acciaioli.

The incontrovertible nothing of us –
But as one other's nymphs and syrinx
Once languorously dancing in the mist;

Time ago (snow)
Talking in the trafficked thoroughfare
Replying to my challenge
'You are a nymph, my dear';
Otherwise I had not used the word.
Now like the violin singing in the strings
Always with her near animity the word,
Sighing as I would, thinking her in the serenade.

The serenade which alone lasts after all this time,
Like once in a mere poem of music
Frozen brightly with the red winterless
Snows of Rachmaninov.

FROM: THE GEMINI EXTENSION:
END MY SONG, TANKS OF CAMBRAI

(I thought widgeon used to sit near here
When the marsh was clear).

Before I could find the access to the closed
Paint factory (and leaving Mr. Degringolade trying
To sell his sleepmobile to a man in brown dungarees)
I found the deviating road along which I had once
Carried home the unpainted house-lamp standard
We had just bought in Kilburn. Then I woke myself
Again to realize that the violet mercury vapour light
Was on the other side of the paint factory, the side
Where my Aunt's shabby funeral cortège had gone along
With its one old car and hearse:

Now full of other people awaiting their funerals
Obliviously gaily, with more flowers destined to die
On them as well. And Aunt not only dead remaining
In that unidentifiable coffin.

As some
Self- destruct, others abrade
Our moatlessness with non-
Sense, with armlets swivelling
Free!

Spartacus, the Regiment!
The water ran soft
Between Rotherhithe and Mortlake.
My murderers with the black armbands
Like the armillae of the tower of Siena
Came on the place of plagues
That used to be with me under the yew tree
Lost as the village of Oseney
Crescent.

Kegs of scarabs, armorial beetles; closet prayers as una-
Like as two pleas, word prefect, scuffed and grazed
With finishing touches.

There with the throne's tow
Our royalbargees tight behind the royalblue fugleman
Stole the fanfare show in a brace of bitter shakes.

IN THE JACUZZI KARAOKE GISMO OF REAL VIRTUALITY

(Real title has conversely to be a
SPOT DUB ON FINALE)

Like a mellow wood dry in afternoon sunshine
He settled in comfort sleep before the night time,
His night time, after, after the rainbows. Leapt from 'teens.

The wide quake gap opened throughout
The thoughtless suburbs, running
through thousands of semis
Where nothing like it or anything
else was ever thought of.

They uncondensed from out of the houses
Clap-collapsing, and crowded over the overcrowding
Unscattering spewed into the open upheavaled spaces.

(Before the furnace of the crematorium
They had seen to it that there came
The anaesthetic of death – formally and formerly –
Unless and until death *were* to come
In the crematorium of the Earth-life's disaster).

A leopard leapt green eyed clawing
Out of the black-webbed
Cupboard of our bad dreams,
Surrounded by red curdled sunsets;
And death was suddenly more serious in the suddenly
Unforgetting moment in trivia. Leptotenes.
Fault of thin genes – .

ELAN IF NO BUD TOPS

(Leptotenes are the very fine initiating lines of the opposing chromosomes of
both parties as they await their 'wedding' within the formation of the
originating cell of the new being)

FULL OF EASTERN COMPROMISE

I let the sighted wing tip tip
The now unseen stone again
As now I unsaw Mandalay
Below, opening up no guesses for prizes
But full mindful, still, Burmese,
That star-set star-stone's
Wide-faceted scenes, silentless gongs –

As landing in the hammock under this afterglow
And autumn lime and mulberry ochres
Dabbling; and the heating iron oxide of mosaics
Circumjacent – the compost heap's wet
Interleaving thongs.

If there were just the same a toppling of stars
Under these stones here the same
As under that stone squinnied
The sequinned starry nacres
Of Buddhist temples are!

But when I shall now slowly unturn
From this stone here –
From under the dappling leaves of the rockery
In these less than few paternal acres –
There are the unleft stars of distances brimming
Not unindigenously still here;
And far is very far from far.

COUPERIN AND THE SUBLIMELY
MANGLED CATAWAMPUS

After all these waning ages,

The beyonds of yesterday's temples, who

Do you think you

Are, to pose as another man – ?

The lost art of shy mischief's sly

Elegance, her face against the faintly

Even pale green frieze of the nineteen tens;

Hearing her saying I can't help thinking

Of him wherever I am, of him

Thinking – .

(And wherever is there wherever

The gloriously unlugubrious

Himalayan zeniths are

In an everlasting high of noon,

Regimented snowbound prominences

Breasting proudly bare;

And the ranging Appalachian eminences,

The Cheviots with their up-reaching peaks:

As merging and beyondly high

They equitably all dragoon

To join the beyond-high galaxies

With their all above-rejoicing cheeks).

The way they laid

Siege to my tribute

Was for me to moot that if

As they thought
No more reward
There was to come of afterlife
Then they were all-too-painlessly well paid.

When I re-flew
The row of open beaks
Was not even a nested few –
School names became convolved
With work ones;
And so still I thought (eye-
Catching) I was the wonder
Of my age, till what was in the eyes
Reproved with leaks
Of tears
What was the real scoring of the years.

Where everything returns to everywhere
And in the same place makes its stand
Tristan is Tristan
Is Isolde
And I am the opposite of my nature,
I hold in my mind's hand
That which I am not held to hold.

OCTOBER DEVOLUTION

They called us Octobers
We who stopped well short of wanting
It to be Christmas. In those days sober as
A child, I saw a tumbril in the early dawn
Mist taking human remains down Cleveland Street, that came
From the operating theatres of the big
Hospital in Goodge Street
Up to the Zoo in Regents Park
For the animals.
        For the animals to what?
For the animals to eat – what do you think?
Or so all along I was told.
Is it any wonder that before I was old
I never believed in Father – *Whats*isname?

Now that all that's left of faith and beauty's love
Is given up to nescient mass bemusements,
Terrorist wars, some Maastricht scam,
Or the thin thrills of populist religions
Phonier than even the Established ones –
        What 'Established' ones? –
The unfailingly unavailing
Hot gospelling cold calling ones,
What do you *think* ? –

And all along, time in time out, with the maribou
Fossicking in Angola under moon;
Unfresh from Sevilia – but with a sonrisa – in Malabu,
Or woolfing it in Florida's Orlando
With a sunrise tequila:
I disowned goals in the daylight saving
Of a man
Who always washes his car at his daughter's weddings:

Quite as undreamily I saw the battery yesterday
Again of the once
Installed 3.7 workaholic
AA guns below a Cumberlanded hotel and marbled
Arch on the right side of The Park.
Because I, octobering with the colic
For Hallowe'en, can not sleep these coming Xmas nights.
And then I dreamt more, walking still,
Backwards to a country-fabled
London war-snow Christmas blitz
And forwards to a Turner-
Like alikeness of a Samhain backlog Yule,
With a winter's redsun Norfolk mill –
Its grey and frozen-faded water wheel.

SONG FOR PUTTING THE DUVET COVER ON

Why's it always got to be me – ?
The corner goes into the side
When one of the other one's
At the wrong end
With my tether
And then the first one comes out
While one of the *other*
One's into the wrong corner
Until it also escapes
And I'm going to give up
In all this dither
(And while positively clouds
Of commensal house mites
Encharm all the pillow and lung slips
Because it will all have to go
Right for wrong in the end
When we're supposed to be
Tucked up under the cover's ticks).

ASMODEUS THE TORTOISE

Come with me under these dark
Woodlands.

For next it was the siege of the plover,
The sparring skiamachy of leaf-left
When kinked were the autumn stems,
After the twists of come-look-alive-with-me
Burgeoning riposte, after aestivation
In turreting cloud hills.

Then I looked out through the snow smoke
Of a lime day, incarcerated
In moss-packed opal – yes, too,
I lurked under the flapping blanchisserie
Of a May-day –

And for all the gaunt hoping in shining
And louring, was devoured in my shell
By hope of merciful tidings,
By hope of a newly acceptable complexion
On things.

A polatouche flew
Between the almond blossom
And the blue;
The squirrel flew over the garden
Of holier than unholy loves.
And I could put my head out
Onto the blesséd block
Of the lettuce's leaves
Again.

A (– COCKNEY) COCKTAIL OF TWO CITIES

I was by the Rue
Du Faubourg Montmartre
As if in the shadow
Of an Art
Deco gin palace
From the Nag's Head
At Holloway,
While it imparted
The odd impulse
To buy
An ice-shaker
For cocktails (and a loaf of bread).

How was it the London boneshaker
Trams from old clanked there
As I saw traces of sawdust spray
Round the doorway corners of the Cité
Bergère's brasseries, late noon that day – ?

And it was only that morning early
We had been rattling through Creil,
With the Sacred Heart's mound
Already rearing up summer-sunnily
Ahead, and the train's jingling
Sound –
Like a couple of sous in our pockets – :
Or was it, as we passed, a Doppler of signalbox ducats
Mournful-recedingly jangling?

You said we'd be just the same, wrangling
Amiably by the Welsh kingfisher stream
As usual, and
When home-was-foreign was also home again,
Though we only thought we'd come
Back to it in
Its old familiar name.

AFTERNOON BIRD

Ancient of days, feeding the hand
That bites you
Clumsily-lovingly.
Afternoon bird.

In the half field, middling in a small Wiltshire town
Next again, in the same place, same time
All life –
The railway bridge in summer hot sun afternoon,
The weed out of the glowing age-pumiced brickwork,
By stifled unwaving goosefoot
At the ground of arches; deserted of people as far
As the sleepy bird's eye can see, as far as the crowsfoot
Flies in the unstirring drowsiness.

And in
Such a flash
I shall fly
With all the other birds
From out of a winter night's belfry,
Past her our moon

With the many knowing gorgelets of outworld,
Miranda of the Uranus moons,
Goblets of ungone-out fires.
At the end of all these days.

At the end of the beginning.

AND SEE THE WORLD

The slab-side lane my willow weeps alight
Unrippled night red-yellower without the city's smoke
A pale evensong of past innocent days
A wall and hollyhocks sun-mixture.
Bowled from the nursery's end
Where a child is older then his father
All out for 21 – not rather
Nel mezzo del cammin di nostra vita
From Piccadilly to Leicester Square
Odeon
A distant prospect of London Town.

A slatternly jilt carousing crakes
A corn again, proffers gorgeous promise,
Genesis, but expecially parthenogenesis,
Unthought; siquis me sinat usque basiare
Then nictitated disillusion, home thoughts
From a bawd.

Five webbed skies flat with cirrus tails;
The ploughed field, an overwatered sun avails.
Alberich and Hagen – how to get the Ring
That is the question. First the leaf and then
The oak. Comme des nuées flottent gris les chênes.

Of wormwood furniture a bed's head facing east:
The Washstand; a general air of snug cleanliness
But snug. There are some trees outside,
The sun's wan glimmer, and a cloudless pane
Of staying in bed. And two get up.
They've said their prayers. We weep to see
So soon fade away, omnis cellula e cellule.

Chitter-chatter in a wind-washed drum
Curlew croaking on a windy plain
Air-walk past a lover's house
To dream of Titian, Gaugin, Matisse.
Where to, Sir? Hampstead Parthenon, please.

SHADES OF SABRINA'S QUARRY,
SPELLS FROM ISLAMEY AND COCKAIGNE

Little the golden
Filigree clock turretlet
Still with Balakirev, Kazak and
Samarkand,
Camden Hill (How can you have recognized me
in the jungle of my fortuitous growth,
through yours?). Towerlet
Of clock Prokofiev
From hospital history casements onto
A salopian hill of river school
In amongst green vamp fronds, spring in winter,
Warhol, Della Francesca, Lichtenstein –

Later, latest life
Co-ordinates fronting now leaf-before-letting
Spring's blow, was foremostly formerly-now:
A mutton-bone vertebra school towerlet
Child-eyed
Ominously wild-eyed, life-far reaching.

Everything went wrong
For this to lie more
Than dreams all right.
You life will be as the fruitful vine of
Your wife (oh yeah –), and your house will be
Like one up for sale to support someone
Helpless in a heartless nursing home;
Thy children like years of dying olive branches.

I keep my nightmares to myself.
I have to.
They are for keeps.

CANDLEMONGERS

But the autumn who warns his finger
On my recollecting rote's bell ringer
Changes the house sides, the brown light's blighter
Motes infill across wintering city streetyards.
Slow, the lurch-sprightly streetwise lamplighter
Prinks sedately the toply peeping standards
Of this mazy cake of a town, and the whiter
Dull-blown smokescreen's meagre shower sieves
Flecks round the night-down flarelets, thieves
The last seeping of afternoon to the late sentiments of wind,

In murky crescents, lurky and terraced
In downstep depths: none dare touch
Them hardly till slack jaw harden with the ginger zest
Of yellowly inflicted frostbiter,
Cruelly affable after the last crusts of harvest:

And then oblivious leave them to their own mind – ;
The night-reeking eyebrights smarting close
Before the acidulous thirst of cold much
Pulverize the lamellae of all these, my mementoes,
And destabilize the atheroma-elder's clutch.

Still, so, I know the years' candles afforestate my ice –
The eternal taper-roundsman shares his lightship –
And life's lengthening electrifying shocks, love's heady blackouts,
All slipped cables of karate'd arteries, clots and clouts.

Winking before the scission is this time libation's slip
Of a sub off the past, blinked as the coming scroungerman's lice,
Connivered as the lovingly prinked prickings
On my first short pastry cake or Robin's snow hop trackings.

Ah, but if the introit of Michaelmas fumes
In suns of white savouring, waking Spring's
Pullulating rouncival or Ember Days' dooms:
My flavour of these cycles unsacked by the last bobtail
Who deftly flees the night air, consumes
The summer birthdays' cake and ale:
Withal, I'll deafly not let fall the word which makes my painting
Of another autumn need for sun and winter in my hungry fainting,
Though should I seem drank to in fat years
Or forsaken in a beggar's vale of tears.

SPIRIT OF THE LIVING DEATH BEHIND KING'S CROSS STATION

Let me ask you a few very sinful questions.

Do you remember the one veeringly bestirred

Black bird that flies outside, behind

The black railway terminus semicircular sun-high

Window aloft with roof heat and soot shimmering

And still flies from that roof on a relentless sun-blistered

Day, a day black with sun-nowadays? And yet it flew

In the gasps of still-olden air towards where you

Lived as a child in the grey and sunnily down up there

Away, sun-suffocated: do you still live it that way?

Do you remember where you were

When President Caesar Threnody's wife was shot?

(I wonder if I may take this broken old second-

Hand suit case back to another smoky-sooty platform

Of many years ago – where there was to be a dread

Railway accident in twenty years, though -- and that

Itself is nearly ten years ago – : back to

A completely lonely platform, void of its last wistful

Ill-affording holidaymaking few; the platform alone

Now, or then, as it must seem, waiting for a tunnel-from train?).

Did you remember who you were going to be,

President Caesar Threnody,

When you found that plucking maids of Kennet and Thanet

Wouldn't bring back Cornelia? – wasn't that it?

Long ere the MeDallus Cimbers hatched the Pontine Plot
Across Romney's not yet ruptured marshy spot
You flew over into me when I was playing fusion
In this King's Cross black comedy
To be beside myself in the Bay of Hernia,
Combining all with fervid love of Rachel
Prejudice and every glacial
Hatred here, and whether in Andromeda Imperia
Or Imperial Cataluña:
For all you did for you did for Calpurnia.
And you took on with your style of flair
The mantle of the living death above suspicion,
Of the living wife beneath arrivederci Roma,
And beneath Il Duce's splendid Statione Termini.
So, Et Tu, Caesar! – Wake up, my little Caesar!
Your memory's playing tricks with me.

THE TREATY OF ALL EXPEDIENT REVUES

In all, all in the petrol-tappy leathersickly car
To the bitter buttercup parks of thicketty low
Tall grasses and parsley wildernesses, out on a spice
Of dandelions summer cemetery picnic.
So go we, cats' baskets for hampers
On the child-sat running-board,
A child forced to be too Christian for the occasion,
By sternly barely unbending avuncular emissionaries.
Thus, reverend unconformist Jim pulls up,
Far from the over there bee-loud
Honey-acrid grave's flowers,
Where we all hardly think, even reproachfully, it is
Still poor bloody infantryman Harry's.

Not exempt of flaws, then either, I will then offer you
Park gates open at night, sadly railinged to
Behind shrubberies – but softly asking within. I will give
You the further railway curve liably bedding
Under its palely scalloped awning, its jutting narrow
Running roof – yes, in its unthundery blueing, blueing,
Under its muffled starry and motionless shedding.

And I will more burlily
Give you a sputtering moped buff
Bluffly-vanishing-echoing slowly rowdily
Less and less rough
Along a Normandy out-of-village empty street grey-
Wetly, spring-wintery in eternal pre-petit déjeuner earlily.
And I will give you the rest –

the rest that is so well prosecuted in the low
Plain cubes of rooms, squares with white
And green to low inside outlines, set by winter-wide
Shallow estuaries in silent summertimes.

EITHER/OR

Like Kierkegaard,

    Whose thoughts,

        "Amorphous (a recluse –),

            Abrogate desire:

                A 'masochistic' ruse;

                    And censure nature".

                        Like mine–

                            Oft times egregious

                                To another being,

                                    An empyrean sophrosyne!

                                Or shudder, pain

                                      As Rimbaud, Mallarmé,

           To hang modestly   Verlaine:

                Those thoughts   Poor anodyne–

Poetastic? – maybe,   On this proemial

    Even to me,   Coenosarc:

        But, to outfill:

            Éclaircissement! Tempered

                With the long supple

                    Esemplastic stems of grass

                        On a greying summer hill

                          With the thunder's breeze

                            And SAK (even without I)

                              With no painkilling saki;

                              But an internecine

Excludingly,   Function

    Yet with all to a   To think

        Consequent, and gladly,   Frustrated-

            A process intermingled sadly.

AS IT USED TO BE GOING TO BE

Let white on blue endure,
Escape the finity
That is not sky
And white land,
With white clouds
Against the blue above the air.

Show me the why and way of it.

When the high wind volleyed
And guardian the moon was
I was castled in quietness
Begazed and slurred I was

And I heard
I heard the myriad thrill
Of holy and boon
Of the whisper of the lieder
In the philosophic strings.

And the bow of the lovely
Played me to sing –
All me was therefore re-resonating.

And then it was thereafter
That the green light shifted
Over our first form
Through afternoon columbine
And evening lime
Still from
The lamplit night trees of childhood.

So then all we contemplated
Within all of we
Something surely belling within
The heart of hearts;

Moonlit with creatures
And shape of toy
Till love from old centuries
Overslept the boy.

ENTERTAINMENT: MY OWN WURST ANOMIE

Their anthrax outlived them, left their quicker-smothering malaise
(Just as I did my multicoloured
Swatches of bustickets, all redolent
With chewed tobacco and blue petrol
Smoke and many-boot dusty, brought
Ticket by ticket to a secretly calumniating conductor
By visiting uncles – chilled by their above-me halitosic arguments and
Their free gifts – culminating messages,
Missing links that weren't lost as meal
Tickets for what would have been – sustaining me –
My mash and sausages).

And just as I seemed to outlive them (– a self-succouring feint),
Forgetting then all coming anthrax days
While I revelled in the haunting paint
Smell of wrapping-new engines, which would be
Much collectable today, I was tolerably
Even reminded then of how a broken arm, –amid us, fecklessly
Surviving, could mean a broken Christmas.

My anthrax outlived with me even there, dormantly staved in
The Christmas tree I would have caught my glowing germs
From, from the cynically incubating needles of pines;
They thoughtlessly caught their killing glow-worms of ptomaine
From broth made out of the sawdust of an ivory piano
Key factory, near the cattle market just by Camden Town.

Christmas comes but once
And the rest is a bitter trounce
Of remembering the wasteful warmth
When the fickle killers abided
With us into the everlasting fields.

Twinkle twinkle little star
Save this sheep with a ha'porth of tar.
There isn't so much longer now to go
For it all to go on seeming so long ago.

TACKLES AND TUMULTS OF MORE HAPPENING TIMES

Two shadowly move by the door and a doctor
Lastly coughs. The final yashmak'd anaesthetist
Gloatingly fingers the valves of his dirtiest
Trick gases, and a hypodermic like a masked
Humming bird props me up dancerless
As a wailing wallflower to the life.
I suspect then much; then some, – then more.
Thou shalt not die without living it
Down, all this.

(I was in the end surprised
At the people who in the event made
Up the company of my life –
Although I knew that could not come
In any other way, the way its happenings blended).
White railings in unexpected places,
Half-way up low-line white walls
On the grey Belgravia side of Pimlico.
Times that will be in mind when mind
And all is dying, like views of simpatico
Youth, when that and that was what we were;
But as for me I might as well not have been there
For them that were there, the girls who were then
À la mode –
Clumsily not unasked.

But thus; and because thus even more
Then; and after (and before)
We were there, in the lost-out young first
Of my here today and gone
But elsewhere away,
Of my one and not nearly
Not only time.

A CHANCE TO DREAM OF RETAKING YOUR OWN PASSPORT PHOTOGRAPHS

Peaches and cream or whatever is your perishable tipple:
    When I could just undiscover
In the my harsh hooligan music of a Buxtehude kirk
    The cut to the stiff upperlip of the peak
Of widow's weeds, showing they had been got at
    Up the garden path; 'she twisted her fingers
Into the mortice deadlocks of her hair'.
    The you-there is beautiful – wish the weather were here – .

When again reincarnate, we were sunnily
    Of the naturally reverse in that fronded family.
And I am like the merchant seeking goodly pearlwords no-one
                                  deprecates,
    All so long not ago; who never left anything on other people's plates
So that he can outnumber you from the substantiable decadent pit
    That some one might want to keep depravedly outcast in
By making an agon-bite non-permit
    Of the hands that fed him
Instead of selling all that there was to purloin
    Of pride, self-redeem of contactable hermit
Out from the festering overtures of the contemptible old-familiars
    When I am too unsecurely tired to securely smoke.

I don't know why I keep on doing this waviness
    You don't have to take my words for it to get your sums right
In the bespoke saleslady's stampede: to be clobbered by security videos
    Just like the perfect scream exit visas and magicomedy
Snapshots, in the real-time-value customers' excise

Of restrictive measures, reprimand of punctilios.
I feel the wind on my skin because it just untouches my testy toes
  With apparently that noctilucent cloud, always the run-up
To the running-down, knocking you devourably sideways as it overawes
  With hungerlove. Lord keep me calm as a clock
On strikerlight with all these it just happens with milt of roes
  To do justice to, because the meter reader has given me
The final notarized waivers, disclaiming all contumely of customs –
  But they're going to break in under the Act, rowing their ova-oars,
To cut the juice off my premium bombs.

  And am I not glad or sorry of the release
From these obligations and ratewrench demands
  Of finding burdens of resolves for words
When I and my trappings shall only seem dead
  And all the balanced things will come at once for ever again.

HOUSE OF ARENEIDA

Now, there will not be enough time left
For me to be ill enough to be able to get into
My old suits again.

These are these fast removing days
When the foreign logo on the lid
Of a jar of imported marmalade
Is the same as that of the name
Of the road up the road
In this home country town
Of exile from home town.

When it is now next to die not
Next to the espoused still of girls,
That warm of eye and hair reclaims
A-still from there, as from all other waysome
First wove dearly webs and dearly toils,
Those close bequeathings that must still have come
To come from firstly pose of figure of maternity.

'I knew a lover unknown to the nations
Unstale in the rounds of my saint sacrary;
Worshipping his trodden ground given to me,
Favoured with their exheredation ere his death:
Never a drawcansir in the cotoneasters' breath.
Now in this hermitage, seeming mine of our name,
Age-old alimony of the channelling libations:
His song in my obsequies, groves of my veil-taking duals,
Hoping out of the spandrels of my spare handfuls
To make a silent exedra of his fame'.

HELVELLYN VIA HOHENZOLLERN AND HYÈRES

A (confused-) trainee courier's there-and-back romp, and more.

Dying dolls of a dusty sail but just

As red as when the unsawn hollow mast first half-seas

Folded on it, all pre-scented from boutiques de St. Honoré

Near the chanel isles. So your rebutting ship comes porting

Home, only for you to board a ferrying train, for Lake

Hills on high. The cumbriasome engine is rusted from tyre

To dome, if not so shrill-squealingly one imagines as

That just before then and long before

Pulled you from Dieppe and puffed you into the Gare St. -Lazare.

It somehow reminds with all its olds into the thenly new

Of the caravanned fair dynamos you could with as much

Assault of motherlove earths get your Hampstead Heath into

For showman's toffee. And memory dynasties of despotic dead,

Shades of your remembering downcast ethnographies, hop, cheek

By happy jowl, within your poor trajectory, all there's to here,

Ingenious as this borrowed wordsworth of a railway to Grasmere.

For it might not have been of as wide a gauge as such former

predestinies

As the Spanish running from Irun by Hendaye,

But more like to J.S.Eisenach handing down Brandenbergs,

Margrave to Mozart, upper-lipped over Habsburgs I would rather

Not have to forget with Wiener's Sacher poppycake and fig-prinked

Coffee. Not for a moment to exclude those very first clover-cows

Seen on the pristine pilgrim's way to face Fenélon

And Fragonard, steaming through Neufchâtel

And Forges-Les-Eaux to the salade de tomates cheapness
Enforced by hard-upness in the square by St. Sulpice.
(Or to the ghosts of me my familiars as I at Versailles
Spent myself fast awake by the Petit Trianon, or likewise
Had my elbow tugged by others yet anon
Like the disappearing rollicking-ravager soldiers
On the shaming-pleasure rocketing-reprimanded invasion beaches
Of the Wehrmacht Dieppoise).
And then after all reality of made-up rearing abaft
The chimney-breasting engines, dull-bellying schooners
Under mackerel clouds, going reflected in the shoals,
From Windermere again, until with the Mistral of Provence
To Bandol on the instant you are arriving,
Jangling out from the marshalling yards
Of Seine-et-Oise, arriving, yes, for not yet another
Last time, at the unfreshly un-flesh gagged, the prodigiously
Divine atoll of the Île du Levant.

REM REMEMBERING

I have dreamt just then of a place I could not
Place when I was awake, trying to remember where and when
Was it and I, in that slightly-raised-railinged-pavement
Brown and seedy pub, over a cloudy lorry-throbbing main
Road (and there was more than a suspicion of tarnished brass
Rail and mangy plush in there – when I had got out).

It's all where I seem to have bought a winey drink
For a dark-skinned girl (engaging eyes locking quickly into
My moving eyes, now, again, as I'm looking), and I know
I got myself a half of bitter (only a half, I remember –).
And then we went out, and there was some question of money.
And parted, after two goodbyes, and wondering about buses –
Only we seemed to have met friendlily before, if even just
Before (maybe at some business conference along the way?).

As I dreamt it, I remembered an exactly parallel dream in my
Dream, and it seemed to me that I was really dreaming
And then remembering having dreamt what once had 'really'
Happened. But, awake, I can't recall the full frame
Of its actually occurring (although I strongly feel it did).
What do *you* make of it?

(REM   rapid eye movements during dreams)

THE WATCH-WIDE-WORLDS OF GUILT

She thought unthinkingly we must get out! – get out of town,
Before the lights go up, and then remembered
All the time that they were *having* to put up with
The Joe Macmurdles's ciné of stills and that she
Was next door to next-door-the-other-side's
Nearly as utterly bored M'sieur-Dame Falconbrides
('That gaff-blown schooner – to the gunwales down!').

Everybody throws the book in them at you –
Whether their snapped estuary is silted up with crawfish
Or our boiled tourists like cracked molluscs
And without a snapshot beginner's luck
(-Without a stitch? –)
Film the nudist rifleman go swan-shooting;
And she is like a beach-bag postiched Leda
We can't rightly see
And he is another 'delight of the muses'
Pastiched out of Crashaw
(So afterwards you said – that's Rich).
Tedium of other people's private fascinations, horridly mesmerizing
Even if you can't get yourselves also into their pictures – .
The unshared holiday and the unfair strictures.
How long with the blower off till the apparatus fuses?

All all the ignoble of glaring beachgames, surly
Whelks and shrimps, sultry slides and prints
(I don't think I could stand seeing her
In that monokini again, mud or no mud).

It's a jumble – that we see straight is all my eye.

Pack clouds away – just don't try

Too hard with the fly-by-nights of your finger dints

In grabbing the remote frame advance and focus control.

The hobglobulins are moving in –

And welcome the day when the lights go on again

All over the doldrums of the de-Europeanized plages.

(What's this? Rape of Lucretius – ? Tears in the nature

Of things, heads a bit touched by sunburn – or milk

Of human unkindness; too many saveloys, too much erdbeertorte

And the disguises of topless exposés

Are breaking out all over).

That's it. Put the projector away for another benighted day

With the cable to bind it in place for another rotten year,

And for God's sake don't let anyone (lens-capped –) ask

If they took any *movies* the vacation before last

(I don't really suppose – I can't bear to look

Back – that I really heard

Their holiday friends Borgia and Bess

Sob into their beer when they showed

That one they all took

Of the Pope laying hands on the excavator for reliquaries).

SHIPMATES DIDN'T PASS IN THE NIGHT

Restful chimneypots full of windlessness stories
Of what and what I was, loveglanced across a clouded room.

Acrorst a clahded room
Will they take the armchairs out of the window Calypso
Or let the Achaians suffer from Bosphorus burns
Of Greek Fire, off Ithaca, drifting towards the Marmora:
I thought I saw a shot fly over the bloodyless Dardanelles
While Leander left the manning of the shore-mounted
Torpedo tube batteries to the Turks, warning one of our subs
Of a rushing tin fish salvo; Hero
Lovelorst acrorst a deep sea boom.

I looked at the hammer
And wondered if it knew it was going to be
Hard hit on the nail, and that it would suffer
And be different – but then it wasn't only a hammer after all,
Any more than me, and the substance of the blow
Would alter as we all of us grow
Close here and there constructively
Oversmoothed in the general flow.

Extol the fields while there is still time.
Each infinitesimal contains infinity, one is in fact
The One and partlessly: the pinhead semblance so
Comprehends every coming formula and fugue, even
So seeming still awaiting perceptions, which have to be,
To be made, still, in the foreseeing purpose whole.

Affable grunts the brushing painter to the watcher behind
Retrognathously tucks the bedder
In the chinlessly wonderlost necking
Of the pillow into the case.

WORDS OF DIFFERENCE

Fauve the   Welsh
    moon comes in   curvilinearing
       the silver silk   hill backs and to sleeken the rough
       from the   coast   trees
    and the might   of the Biscay main
    When nobody   but the stoat
       sees in   the small
       hours   uncandlelit

It is   the same
    houris   sphere of the toads'
       fore   stalling, of the blue
       noon   of freedom satsumas
    of a   southern
garden   and the Var corniche.

The theme   tune of
    the swan   song of the jumbo lumber
    floundering Jack   and the jet-over
       I   wouldn't give
    a brass   rubbing
    for a   money monkey landed with
You're all right   jackanapes.

Look in   on Cotman's
    Spinney   when you're next
    down   and out that way
I'll bet   the time of
your   light out my bottom dollar
    over   the Fallodden
       Beaches   or was it Falaise,
    Arromanches?   the Caen sneezing
stone rests in   this Abbot's House bless you.

WHAT PASS THE CAN THE MATTER BE?

If what is true is as I (me, loomingly
Wishing for roots in the germinal gardens of stars,
Me, Fisher the Peterman, stealing the prey
Of Alcedo the Kingfisherman
Kingfishering with his javelin):
Then truth is also that wonder of me stepping alone
On the waters, till unmightied by main, too seeming-easy
In the rear mirror of my days.
But even then I was to go warming my hands, lying
And betraying not to give the Man away, cocks crowing
Their heads off (– 'I never knew him' –). And there came
With good cheer from the cross-tree of cruelty and hate
Familiar words into the flippant gills of our Easters,
Our Springs; and I hear them now in my long-after weeping –
Words staying I still uplift
This sinking plant of you, succouring your roots as if with
Azotobacters
Propounding life, keeping out the blue fingers
Of cyanosed spine tinglers:
And so, keeping the planets in the thinking
Air, you can make it from the moon
Of the Piccolomini
With the galaxy at the garden gate.

From: THE PICTURE BOOK AND THE OTHER PICTURE BOOK:

NAUSCOPE

There are living lamps of fishes

In the splendid tropic seas

Fierce piscatory brilliances

In green liquescent glass, lampreys

Embellished with bright coloured lights,

Cannibal Nimrods expiscating blacknesses

With pelagian dabs and cyclops crabs

And octopus spying in sea-bed bights.

Of unimagined mysteries

And fearsome hatchet claws,

The goblin-headed denizens

With maw-headed jaws:

Hooked-snout Angler fish

With trancing, trailing flames,

Where the deep-sea squids shun the wave rapids

And the murmuring mains and anemone plains

And shark that regale with stories of whale;

Here the grey lamdoidal drifting fish

Search and keel in the bottomless deep

Whilst the lithesome rays go their several ways

With emerald lanterns flashing, frictionless sleep,

In the dim high-pressure beds.

And the conch-clad creatures with red-lipped features

Dangle long antennae, blue-eyed meteorites,

Vying with chela of bathysphere sprites

In coral torch gala for a tentacled whaler:
Armoured thrust feelers in cobalt calm.

In Indian liquid blueness
Far in the rubicelle sea
Blunt and streamlined monsters twirl
With dark serenity.
In the depths where no daylight finds
The luminous faces, there phosphoresce traces
Which halo vert tendrils in hyalose murk.
Here Oneirodes Niger swim
And gondolas, seriatim,
Cressets blazing aquamarine
When shoals of midget fish convene.

Off Afric's coast is the domain
Of Macrostomias, awe-engendering,
Dragging his lanterns, a golden chain
Under the lour ocean their lustre rendering.
Pennants of painted aquarium sprats
Of dull intensity in alcove immensity
Sport their radium fins with the murderous djinns,
Over ochreous shades on the pressurized sand.
And the unearthly waters under the Earth
Entomb the reverberant sky's still density.

For I see round these indefinite stars
When the wild imagined eye no longer stares,
Is regulated to the gloom, I see round them
The electric glow making the deep sea
Into stratified sapphires, and the glistering green
Of fucus and the rufous looming reefs

Into intimate halls familiar as a magellanic vase.

For the cnidocilled nenuphars radiate streamers,

White-fringed in the dumb depths, mauve-inked by the night,

And coil their rippling lashes in the unswelled sound,

Lilies of sea plants sabled from their surfy sky,

The unseen scape wherein their twins the constellations lie

Sought from their celestial bed unrocked: thus wonder I

Midst yellow bathèd lands and small tented saucer strands

Which with faint silver fires down below abound.

THE EAGLES OF THE DAY AFTER DESTINY

O hatless Christ, Jesus Pobre,

A donkey ride to the hill-hamlet of Alicante,

Your very head unthorned

Under the great face-fanged watchbirds of the Cape:

Only that I might find

My diffident thrust come to a crown of thrones;

Gavest shelter for a spear in thy side

To every wight and wain

From Charlemagne and Lascaux to Bert Stevens and Scutari.

O matchless grace-

Lessness of us, that we are not with you, legless

As all the battle-junked matchsellers,

Dumped sacks of one-armed harmonica-players

And lottery vendors, all sick grievers that we can't face

In the furnaces of all their Spanish city street lost corners.

How can I hope to do any better

My hobbling but still savioured and blazing comet

Upside down at the end of my tree –

Only in what was always a feasibly on going trajectory,

Even as the lambs are slaughtered at Easter, with rosemary unctions,

And when the spring-sharp silver paper

Round the bright young eggs has gone for ever,

Gone to be for ever

Unseen to all the up-craning comets of cemetery wry-necks

Blinking at their overheads,

At our thus so poorly attended eagle-cometary functions.

It was the eagle of that crown said

The dream-you, and the ghost-you, are for real

Real you, in homogeny oscillating with all the other you's undead

That are angels in paradise, and still thus of the resolving mole.

And for all that we tend

To like-believe what we most easily take to

We never lose the particular feeling of any day

That was in its then-ness to be so freshly again lived through.

It says it will last itself so, around and through you,

And time has from the first met his avenging enemy,

Has lost his bedevil to the no-time of his life.

All mixed up in the dust of starts, Petrushka;

I keep meaning to ask your forgiving nature

In how much of a lengthless little while

You my ulna will seem to lie or powder

In the rest of the invisible excreta of breath,

Is it just as never not unbelonging

As the impress line of my see-thru' clothes.

To the one body but all-thing, and wayout ideas

Of the one and all body of outflaming synergy?

Let us now and then be association-full and free,

With a comet's eagles of eyes

That your heart can't put your hand on,

That, truth to tell, lie even as they speak,

And eyes that hear, too deep for tears.

SOMETHING TO SLINK ABOUT

In my moral sump of mystery where even freeze-high glycol

(With its wraps on the piston rods of the grey matter rattle)

Is in oil a non-starter: in this my cranky case I built

A torsion clock on the owl of midnight which was all

I could come up with: so I could better time my brain

To see and read this old old mindly-echoing lunar map that was

Yellowed with the tea of tranquillity, of no-man's age

And a picture made of watch parts. Let me then go on

With the more than double life

I am to be well pleasing, if you

Take my meaning here as true and true

To faith; Vercors and tweedle-dummy help me

To the Wohltemperiertes Clavíer

And the Riviera by St. Cyr behind Toulon, I who cuddled

So often the bundle of holly and the scythe

Of the opposite-of-sowman so as to make a clearance

Unseasonable in the crowded Christmas

Tube train so that you would always along

Ago laugh as if you'd bought the first piano-

Warmer advertized for under a fiver in the hyper-

Market until and until if you were

Next to that train at the Barbican

You were when it ran headlong into the infraction

Moorgate end of a tunnel like out of the wrong end

Of an impeded gun, from the muzzle as breech
To make a monument of rescue and flesh
Wreckage, while you were crying on the other
Side of your face, you, born for the underground

Of the harpy hampstead, helping out
You pittance with temporary clerks of Chancery
Too cowardly to give any of your ill-begotten blood.
Time lessens life's demands? You were not right there even if right you
could.

From: CHARON'S FERIAL STORY:
VALE ATQUE AVE

Out of the window the wind cavalcade
Wires the white seagull
Gliding behind geniculate branch-trees,
Fingering the white weather-cock;
The twin twigs above a fancied flood
Of the rain sheet and day mist
Dance, persistent in their red elasticity,
Twigs which, now again,
Scrape against the topmost dry screen
Of my east garden room.
The sepurtured shrike, incurious of ants,
Flies from wood to remote spire.

When the sun was a bright streak on afternoon walls
And the swathe of high corn
Flooded up to the french windows
From the thin knots of ocelot eyes;
When the sun waled lemon and paled
There was again a blue sky and a sea calm,
And the sheltered room, latticed and withdrawn,
Immured understanding minds
In for a moment the peace.

NO REQUEST, BY FLOWERS

In that it is the function of death

To help me not always to lament

As it were on my majority, that

Times have gone, belovedly, for good:

For here they come, as thick as harvest

Sheaves, as another false New Year awaits; and

Not even alone even temporarily here

Am I; and we can all enter on to the adventure

To which this is the interlude

From the last.

A DAY OUT WITH THE BARQUES OF AVON
(OLD SOKES FOR NEW)

Mizzens rose,

Masts before

Their masts of nut

Had sotted yaffles* peened –

For all the sails aloft now honed,

On ocean and this river,

Not sail-less ever

Any more, not staying at home

Like these trees – .

(And while we're

So mischievously busy getting out the boat's best china –

Off to a tease –

Araneidan the spider comes by here

As gung-ho if you please

As shogun weddings

Are, and as ferociously happy as, under the designer-

Roof, sunshaded from rains,

Her intendedly bagged bug remains,

As comfortable as if in a rug's beddings).

Well, 'Life begins at fortitude', I say:

'We go back a long way;

My wife is on fire

Like a flaming harmonium

* *Yaffles* are green woodpeckers.

Homeless from home,
A ladybird yammering
Beneath a barking woodpecker'.

Night came at long last
With a glass of must
For us, touched with hemlock,
And we get paid for it on the way out –
As the Bard gives a final toast
To the villagers (with folkloric snatches from Prufrock),
For never losing a battle before it was ever a won.

ALL OUR NOT-TIME

'I can show you where there are squirrels

In the tree-tops of the old wood – you must

Believe me, I saw them there as a child, in Ken Wood'.

(But I wasn't at all sure they would be there today for us).

But, – and what an unbelievable relief! – there they *were*,

A couple of them, loping along:

And I could carelessly say

'There you are – I told you so, I told you they would

Come for you in Hampstead –

That they would be there for you – '.

(That was a day I played truant from work, as I often did

Then to be with you, and we went across by the Spaniards

Inn before tea in the old Two

Blues opposite the Everyman

Cinema, by way of the rapture

Of being together, going by Ken Wood).

NO GHOST TO LAY

In this quietude of sun dust afternoon
It is not you who sit in the room
In the natural wood of chair
And very wooden room, but your presence, set
With earthenware jar of honey;
And we have somehow to leave there
For some train to catch and yet
Stay youngly as if we had arrived only
Just for always to stay
In the discretely cow parsley
And cretonned calm.

LAST WORD TO HEISENBERG

I am half glad I have at last come
To live round here, in anti-funeral but ardent
Funeralgoing England country, even, where there is little
Heart for lonely mourning of me and last-lost love: where
They live unskulkingly around here listlessly, not even
Trying to make so-called love, but loving lovelessly
Quiet. I am glad, you there, London and Montmartre, I have no
Photographs left from all past destruction of photographs,
Of the more-and-more beloved child-garden pictures; save one –
One which I re-thread with memory lifelongs – just
A corner of a garden showing it all, from whence
It all comes, smudged and bright, as if I who stood there
Knew I stood in the pains of death and birth to come,
To come there, in first home, and here in home's outlast.

THE SWISS CEREAL UNIVERSE OF A
WANDERING JEWELLER

In a long dim wooden granary
Room, with a far red sun slanting in yellow
Between the barrels of the lentils, all the pulses
In the cool dust of the touching-winter shelter
And the chandler colours of old timber, mushrooms
And chrysanthemums, dry leafy clean pungent amongst
The sloping low side beams.

The slow crescent, then besprent with quartz splotches
Along an alone arcade street; funiculars above; Montreux's.
Lake ringside seated under snow peaks. Now though, as
In a black echoing street, no-less-
Livingly in the after-imagery traveller's
Sense. I circle your sweeping bandolier, baguettes
Of shop-shut late nights, fluorspars,
As I circled, will circle, that curved opulent rank
Of High Street shops ostentatious in the canton of Golders
Green, granite-banning as a bullion chandelier of a bank
To a loner, an impoverished loner pockets full of stars
(Which street also has more than its fair share of Swiss watches).

FLAIR OF FIELDS

As whose word should make music,
Experience of words. Nothing counts
But only one night, perhaps tonight:
No crumpets, no home, stopping
Short of home. My self saw the instant
My form, the charred bones and flesh-tree,
Then was vapour and powder; on what shore
The fleecy billets serely rise again.

OCCUPATIONAL DECEASE

What d'you do, when yer not writin' pertry?
I swing on the lamp posts, and roll on the floor.
I knew you blokes wa'n't like us chaps, but cor!
Well, then I'll shout and I'll climb up a fir-tree
And caper and bellow and monkey and flit,
Maybe knock my head on the wall for a bit.
Well, and who'd 'a hever 'a thought that was true!
Well, you wanted to know the truth, didn't you?